Advance Acclaim

Dr. Kozhi Makai brings a refreshing and encouraging look at what we all face in our lives...the many challenges that life inevitably delivers. With knowledge and wisdom of a man more than twice his age, Dr. Makai provides realistic and very thoughtfully seasoned examples, throughout this wonderful book. Born Beating the Odds™ is a masterfully-written, thought-provoking book that will surely help coax, encourage and enlighten its readers through understanding and dealing with life's difficulties. Read this book with your eyes, listen to it with your heart, embrace it with your mind and you will learn a great deal
Tim Carlisle, President
Christ Centered Sports, Inc.

Dr. Kozhi has taken life's simplest concepts and massaged them so that from the simplest of minds to the one without measure, one can sit back and self-reflect
Stefanie Dugan, Administrative Services Manager
City of Oakland Public Works agency

An uplifting memoir of life through example. Enter a new mindset where your faults are treasures and obstacles are paths to a healthy you. Dr. Kozhi Sidney Makai guides us in becoming better at our challenges instead of making excuses for our flaws
Michele DeLoof, CEO
Modern Candy Clothing

I have learned from the school of life that in the face of adversity and against the toughest odds, success is only guaranteed if one keeps his eyes on the big picture! This book is a reminder to focus on the "prize" and not the "process"
Gilbert Lungu, Corporate Account Manager
UUNET

In Born Beating the Odds™, Dr. Makai shows his reader that each man is capable of creating his own destiny and gives him the inspiration to turn that destiny into a reality. He teaches that becoming what you want to be is about first realizing who you want to be and shows how obstacles and heartaches are the necessary impetus for improvement in a person's life and character. By assuring his reader that he is no stranger to hardship, Dr. Makai is able to meet his audience exactly where they are in their own struggles and inspire them to shape their own lives by meeting adversity with an attitude of victory. This book offers an original perspective, applicable to all readers, on how to journey from wherever they are to wherever they would rather be. In reading this book, I have learned more about my true self than I have in many years of soul-searching

Alyssa R. Nichols, Licensed Master Social Worker
University of Texas Medical Branch

I feel like my privacy has been invaded...as though something inside me that I couldn't and didn't investigate has been yanked to the surface and articulated for all to read. The upside is I don't think I'll be the only one feeling this way

Itwi Liwena, Architect
Marseille, France

Dr. Makai's book is a solidly-written, methodical approach to taking on some of life's biggest challenges: disappointment, betrayal, rejection, and loss. Instead of just delivering a "rah-rah" message, he teaches us we have two distinct choices: be a passive victim or hold ourselves accountable, adapt, and become a better person after each experience. His message also reminds us that overcoming such setbacks makes all subsequent achievement much more meaningful. Dr. Makai is likely to become a significant national and international leader. He is gracious to share his thoughts and template for success in his books

Dean Johnson, Division Vice President
Apria Healthcare

There is isn't a single person that will not benefit from reading this book! Young or old alike, it is never too late to take the wisdom from this book and use it to make your life better. The perspective in this well-crafted book is at one point obvious but at the end the driving point that tells you "if it's so obvious, then why aren't you doing it?" Kozhi reminds you that life is tough but you can be tougher. You were born with the spirit to adapt, to overcome adversity, to persevere. You simply have to remind yourself that you can do it. This is not a self-help book but rather a realization book. This book awakens our inner spirit to strive and be the successful person that we were born to be
Sergio Grado, President
Gradco Construction

I could not have read this book at a better time, it does not sugarcoat the adversity, pain, rejection, and loss that we all face in this life, yet it's uplifting and full of faith and hope. Kozhi's writing conveys simple truths that we all tend to overlook in our journey, it's a book that I will pick up and re-read from time to time as a way of reminding myself that I was "Born Beating the Odds™"!
Rick Frank, Account Executive
CoreStaff

Born Beating the Odds™ is a well written account of a young man's journey to better himself through hard work, perseverance and an unbelievable understanding of the world around him. Lessons learned by Dr. Makai are presented and their contribution towards goals achieved are included. This book is an inspiring and thought provoking masterpiece, regardless of the stage that you are at in your life. Those who endure win! This theme is carried throughout the book. The feel of the book is like having a conversation with Dr. Makai
Aurore Larson, Civil Engineer
Kimley-Horn & Associates

...a timeless master piece interwoven with personal experiences and those of many others who went on to become what they set out to achieve with all odds against them. To those wondering as what the answer is to the question about life's summum bonum, let this book swing open the door that will lead you to the conclusion of the matter...

Alex Phiri, Academic Dean
Milton Keynes Bible College (UK)

Born Beating the Odds is an excellent book written in a refreshing and easy to read style. The book spots the real life challenges surrounding the issues of motivation and leadership. Dr. Makai draws deep from within to bring forth unusual inspiration to many a reader. It is a valuable work of art, tipped with great finesse. The author is clearly well read in the fields of business leadership and motivation. He balances expert knowledge with practical examples from real life scenarios, highlighting how, for example, one can deal with such vices as betrayals, disappointments, discouragements, jealousy and envy. The author rises tall in this book, providing some thought-provoking moral and ethical guidance. This book is well-grounded in virtuous issues of moral suasion with ethical imperatives well articulated. This is a highly recommended book for the general readership and for the academicians and students of business leadership, including motivational speakers, audiences of motivational speakers, and anyone with a deep interest in the social sciences and the humanities

Dr. Kenneth Mwenda, Senior Counsel
The World Bank

Born
Beating the Odds™

Also by Dr. Kozhi Sidney Makai

How Can I Come Up?

Culture & Leadership: A Comparison of Cultural Orientation and Leadership Preference among College Students in Zambia and the United States

Born Beating the Odds™

By

Kozhi Sidney Makai, Ph.D

Scrolls & Scribes™ Books
Independence, Texas
www.ScrollsandScribes.com

Born Beating the Odds™, BBTO™, BBTOers™, BBTO Spirit™, BBTO Academy™, BBTO Commencement™, Larger Purpose Thinking™, Higher Level Living™, Maximizing Excellence™, Question Everything™, and Exploitation Opportunity™ are trademarks of The Kozhi® Companies.

Wheaties® and Breakfast of Champions™ are trademarks of
Special K™ is a trademark of the Kellogg Company
Superman® is a registered trademark of Detective Comics, Inc.
Dr. Scholl's® is a registered trademark of Schering Corporation
Burger King® and Have it Your Way™ are trademarks of Burger King Corporation

This book is a work of non-fiction. Unless otherwise noted, the author and the publisher make no explicit guarantees as to the accuracy of the information contained in this book and in some cases, names of people and places have been altered to protect their privacy.

ISBN-13: 978-0-9799891-0-0
ISBN-10: 0-9799891-0-8

Cover design by adWhite (www.adWhite.com)

Printed in the United States of America

Acknowledgments

...no one mind is complete by itself. All truly great minds have been reinforced through contact with other minds. Every mind needs association and contact with other minds in order to grow and expand – Dr. Napoleon Hill

Everything that I have accomplished in life, including this book, is the product of collaboration between many minds. As a matter of course, many individuals comprise the completion of an undertaking such as this one. To list each one would be tedious and offensive, at best. Invariably, someone would be left out and that would be unacceptable to me. Therefore, thank you to every individual and organization that has played a role in shaping my character and demeanor – past and present. I am a sum total of the experiences that have led me to this point in my life...

Contents

Forward

O nce upon a time, a farm boy from Zambia connected with me through the internet and expressed his interest in attending North Harris College. A light bulb flashes in mind signaling how my first admissions website inspired someone across the world to start achieving his dream in the U.S. As an admissions advisor, I've challenged this young man to transform inspiration to action.

This book is a sequel to his first book, "How Can I Come Up?" that chronicles his personal experiences on how inspiration opens doors to endless possibilities. The author dreams, wakes up, and connects the ideal world with reality. He doesn't leave things to chance. My first few words with him were: "Don't leave things to chance because chance is nothing more than a convergence of probabilities in time, and as such, the occurrence of an expected event is uncertain and unpredictable." Dr. Makai works with intent and direction. His success is a revelation of his wholesome character and deeply religious personality. I am deeply honored to write this foreword to his work of constant inspiration.

Whether you are a generation of baby boomers, gen-X or the millennials, his message is unique and can find a place in your heart and mind.

Severo M. Balason, Jr. M.A.
Dean of Student Development
North Harris College

This publication is dedicated to my wonderful "Zamerican" parents: *AAM "Gov'ner" Makai*, who taught me to "*sokola njimbu; muhinyi, mukawana.*" "Take your axe head (character); a handle (everything else in life) can always be found."
George "Senior" Eberly, who reminds me that I have the world by its tail. I just need to direct it!
Edna "Mommy" Makai, the lovely woman who taught me to pray (and never ceases to pray for me); a gift that continues to give. Finally, *Renée "Ma" Eberly*, whose love and compassion are divine. It is my strong belief that every triumph has its facilitators. You each have literally been an extension of God's hand in my life and words will never do justice to my sincerest gratitude.
I love you…

Preface

How do you make dreams come true? Wake up...

Loading my kayak into my vehicle one afternoon, my American dad, George Eberly, articulated a feeling I had had the entire day. He said: "Boy, you've sure come a long way! What would your mama say to you right now if she saw you?" He was so right, for I was thinking to myself: "I had not even dreamed of owning a kayak, let alone spending time during a work week kayaking, before moving to this country." While, for some, this might seem trivial, for me, it was significant...

I am the youngest of nine children; two girls and seven boys. I was born into an amazing family with my siblings now living in London, Belgium, India, South Africa, Mozambique, Zambia, and Thailand. Yet, for many, we are seen *now* and not from whence we came. While I cannot, and will not, speak for my siblings, I can quickly assert that if there is one thing we have done thus far in our lives, it is that we have *recognized* that we've beaten the odds...

This book is not meant to be a recording of my achievements; even though some are recorded here. Rather, this is a book about the *spirit* behind those achievements. This is not a "motivational" book (if anyone asks what you're reading, be sure to let them know...please). This small book is meant to *inspire* rather than motivate. In my view, *motivation gives you a dance; inspiration, however, puts the song in you!* The purpose of this book is to inspire you into action. It is not my intention or my dream for this to be "another" self-help book you read – well, partially read – and no *real* and *sustaining* change occurs in your life.

My hope is that you will look at this book as a reference for the amazing *awesomeness* that is already *in* you. I am, by no means, suggesting a Greco-Roman attitude of thinking of ourselves as gods. I am merely noting the obvious: there is something in the human spirit that defies science or human understanding. There is something in us that inspires Todd Beamer and others to sacrifice for the greater good. There is something that inspires firefighters to run into burning buildings to save lives. There is something in us that pushes us to become – borrowing from the U.S. Army slogan – all that we can be. With that in mind, I know you are awesome because you managed to exit that protective haven called the womb and enter the unpredictable expanse of earth. That's a *great* start!

I have often been chided for my "blind" belief and faith in humanity. I have been told that I need to approach people with more caution before…well…being "me" around them. I have discovered that this is simply not in my DNA. I believe in people; in their ability to make kings and sages or fools and despondents of themselves. Whichever category you fall in, **I believe in you**. It is quite possible that no one has ever told you they believe in you. If that is the case, know that I believe in you and know, without a doubt, that you have a story; like I tell my students: *it just needs to be told*.

Kozhi Sidney Makai, Ph.D
The Woodlands, Texas

Introduction

I believe man can be elevated; man can become more and more endowed with divinity; and as he does he becomes more God-like in his character and capable of governing himself.[1]

Born Beating the Odds™? Yes. *Born Beating the Odds*™. My titles seem to have an interesting appeal (which makes my publicists very happy) but have very deep and significant meaning for me. Much like my previous book, there is a story behind *Born Beating the Odds*™.

The story behind this title begins in undergraduate school and spans about five years. It began in my Human Sexuality course with Dr. Johnson and my Human Development course with Dr. Cruise. The technical and psychological aspects of human growth, development, and sexuality combined with reflective thought were the potent combination that led me to say to my friend Shaun:

> Did you know that at the time of sexual intercourse, a man will generally deposit between 100 and 500 million sperm? Furthermore, do you realize that with a viability of 24 hours (and, technically, *up to* 48 hours), the *one* sperm that *wins* the mammoth "Fertilization Race" has beaten *tremendous* odds? Several hundred million to one odds, specifically...

Now, at first glance, you're probably thinking: "I thought this was supposed to be an "inspirational" book and not a dissertation on human biology and reproduction." You're absolutely right. Humor me for the next few moments, however; for it is not until you understand this "biological and reproductive" *drama* that you will gain the background behind the *title* and *spirit* of this book.

This "drama" is far from over once the *one* sperm breaks through the cell wall of the egg. If you remember from your biology or human health course, the resulting fusion (fertilization) of egg and sperm is called a *zygote*. The zygote, at this point, is still extremely vulnerable since "for various reasons, about one-third of all zygotes die shortly after fertilization[2]." The place at which the sperm and egg meet in the reproductive tract is often unpredictable and requires that the zygote travel some six inches for implantation (attachment to the womb)...a journey that will take between three and four *days*!

Once *you* view yourself from this perspective, it should completely change how you see yourself. I hate to sound too cliché but you *are* a miracle! Not only that; just the fact that half of you fought against and beat several hundred million competitors is testimony to your awesomeness! You are not a loser! How could you be? You went head-to-head against mighty odds – mightier than King Leonidas and 300 Spartans in the ancient Battle of Thermopylae – and crossed the finish line...*first*. You are not "nothing"! You battled for three to four days to travel six inches!

In the preface, I noted my belief in you...

...now you know *why* I believe in you. You have beaten some great odds already. My questions for you *now*, then, are:

- Why not be glamorous about it?
- Why not make beating the odds a lifestyle?
- Why not finish as spectacularly as you began?
- Why not maximize your "between conception and death" time?

Furthermore:

- What has snuffed that strong, endogenic fire to "be" that brought you into this world?
- Why have you allowed the "supposed tos" to govern who you are or become?

I am the first to admit that I don't have the "Holy Grail" to consistently beating the odds. Like you, I have insecurities I struggle with. I have fears that sometimes deter me from fully becoming the miracle I know I am. Just as you do, I deal with difficult challenges financially, emotionally, psychologically, etc, etc, so, I am not one to "throw stones to hide *my* hands[3]". Yet, there is something exciting about realizing that I am *not* the person that the haters, naysayers, and pessimists think me to be.

In the pages that follow, you and I will collectively work at becoming better at beating the odds. So, get your latte, hot chocolate, or tea and buckle up. You're about to embark on a life-changing journey into the heart and mind of what it takes to consistently beat the odds. You've been warned...

<u>Notes</u>

1. U.S. President, Andrew Jackson
2. James W. Vander Zanden (2000). *Human Development*, Seventh Edition, p.73
3. Michael Jackson (1987). *Bad*. Epic Records

PART ONE
The BBTO Spirit™

1. Pain Appreciation

You have been weighed, you have been measured, and you have been found wanting[1]

Have you ever felt that way? *Inadequate? A cut below the rest? Unable to measure up?* What emotions did this feeling evoke in you? Was it self-pity? Dejection? Did you give up? Comfort yourself with the thought that "perhaps it wasn't meant to be?" Or did you simply become angry? Did this anger turn into rage? And that rage into fury? That is, your rage was so great you could have been classified as being insane?

If any of these questions rang true for you, I believe you have the BBTO Spirit™ - the "Born Beating the Odds Spirit™". You have an *understanding* of the pain and anguish that come with rejection after rejection, put-down after put-down, hurdle after hurdle, or discouragement after discouragement. Not only do you have an *understanding* of this pain and anguish, you have a deep sense of *appreciation* for it all.

"Hold up!" you say. "Did you just say 'appreciation' for pain and anguish?" Yes, I said *appreciation*. There are two kinds of people with regard to pain and anguish: those that see it as an *inconvenience* that must be *avoided* or gotten rid of at all costs and those that see it as an *opportunity* that must be *exploited* for maximum growth. Those with the BBTO Spirit™ have an appreciation for pain and anguish because they see an "Exploitation Opportunity™." They recognize that, just like a butterfly or moth fights through a tiny hole to exit its cocoon, we, too, must fight through our perils so that when we are weighed and measured, we are *not* found wanting.

Dr. Kozhi Sidney Makai

A Giraffe's Tale

In the African plains, new-born giraffes learn this lesson no more than fifteen minutes after being born[2]. When they *first* get on their feet, the mother giraffe swings her long legs and kicks the living daylights out of them! Initially, this is a sad activity to behold because we'd expect more tenderness from a mother giraffe that has been carrying it's calf for 14-15 months. Yet, this process continues until the calf learns to get up quickly. You see, in the plains, the calf's protection lies within the herd. This means that it must be able to quickly get up and keep up with the herd. Anything less and it becomes the main course for lions, leopards or hyenas.

Clearly, giraffes have mastered the art of "rolling with the punches" and learning to *appreciate* and *embrace* pain and anguish. I wonder...what is it that makes us shy away from this life-changing experience? Have we become so comfortable in our technological advancements that anything resembling effort must be automated? Or have we reached a point in our history where there is no honor in *first* sowing before we enjoy a harvest?

Appreciation?

To appreciate something is to be *thankful* for it; to have *gratitude*. According to Dictionary.com, appreciation can be defined as: *the act of estimating the qualities of things and giving them their proper value*. Wow! *Estimating...quality...value*. Without turning this into an etymological discourse, let us briefly examine these three terms: to estimate; quality; and value. To estimate is to measure or give esteem to something. Quality is simply the character or nature of something. Finally, value is the *relative* worth, merit or importance of something.

When we appreciate something or someone, we are, in essence, *determining whether the character or nature of that person or thing is worth esteeming and important*. Tying this back to pain, if we appreciate pain we are saying that we see the importance it has in our lives and we esteem it for the worth it brings to our lives. If you remember the definition of "value" above, you might note that the word "relative" is in italics. This is a sign of emphasis; it is meant to emphasize the fact that how we all value things is based on many personal factors. No two people will value something equally. Some might value their children, their work, their dreams, or their world at one level while others might value each of these at a different level – it is *relative* and *subjective*.

The funny thing about "value" is that my subjective view of it does not matter when set against the backdrop of reality. If I were to burn a box filled with $100,000, having *subjectively* determined that the box and the paper on which the $100 bills are printed is not of high value, would that, realistically, change the value of the $100,000? Silly question, right? No matter what I think about the value of the box and the paper on which the $100 bills are printed, the inherent value of that $100,000 is not diminished.

Kicking Against the Goad

Likewise, no matter what *your subjective* view of the value of pain in your life may be, the fact remains that there is great merit and importance in pain. Instead of "kicking against the goad[3]," you are better off waking up to the reality that pain is an essential part of life and the faster you esteem it, the faster you become more of the person you are destined to be.

A goad is a stick with a sharp point or electrically-charged point. It is used to keep oxen in line. It is never the shepherd's desire to harm his animals. It just happens that sometimes the animals do not behave as the shepherd would have them behave. When they fail to adhere to the shepherd's direction, they are poked or shocked with the goad with the underlying message, "Get in line!"

Oxen often don't get the message and can sometimes be stubborn and rebellious. When they have this stubborn and rebellious streak in them, they kick against the goad. When this happens, the shepherd must make the following message clear to the animals: *It is dangerous and it will turn out badly for you to keep kicking against the goad*[4]. For the oxen, it is dangerous because the shepherd will not put up with stubbornness and rebellion for long; the oxen will become t-bone steaks at dinner...

What about you and I? What does the illustration above have to do with you and I? Everything. It is dangerous for you and I to keep kicking against the goad of reality. Offering "vain and perilous resistance[5]," the end result is often bad for us if we do not clearly recognize the role that pain has in our lives. We develop an entitlement attitude that leads our lives into an uncontrollable tailspin that can only lead to certain death.

Your "death" may not be physical but you will see your dreams die before your eyes. This will then lead to you trying to live vicariously through your children. And, for this, your children will resent you and there'll be no hope of a real relationship with them. I don't mean to be a messenger of doom but this is as real as the air you are breathing right now – you may not see it but you know it is there.

Instead of trying to avoid pain, use it as a conveyor belt to your next level of life. I have written my best poetry in pain. I have played my best basketball games in pain. I have developed my most honest relationships in pain. The challenge lies not in *overcoming* the pain; the challenge lies in *accepting* it as a *necessary* and *regular* pit stop as you grow and develop.

Notes

1. Count Adhemar in *A Knight's Tale* (2001)
2. Gary Richmond in *A View from the Zoo* (2005)
3. Acts 9:5. The Amplified Bible
4. *Ibid*
5. *Ibid*

2. The Symbolism of a Sycamore

We must go through the same progression: Chip away what doesn't belong, sculpt our lives and give them form through the people we associate with and the information we take in, allow the rough spots of our lives to be sanded away through adversity and suffering, and then only then, are we ready to be polished and let our power and beauty show in all of its glory[1]

In a recent conversation, I was told that I lead my life like a *hurdler*...I seem to *enjoy* obstacles! I suppose this is a compliment since it is when I am not hopping fences that I know "something ain't right." I am uncertain as to your pedigree but mine is wrought in so many hurdles that I have come to "wonder" when things are "a little too easy." Some of us seem to be, like Job lamented: "Born to trouble as sparks and the flames fly upward[1]". For some of us, we don't wake up to a Special K™ breakfast; we wake up stretching and warming up for the hurdles we must vault.

Honestly, I don't *know* any different. I don't know what a life of ease and total leisure feels like – that is, one that has not first encountered the requisite suffering or sacrifice. I don't know how to gain anything of value without having to *fight hard* for it. Getting to the princess without slaying the dragon is foreign to me. Reaching the summit or pinnacle by helicopter and not by foot brings knots to my stomach; my mind and body scream: *"What's the catch?!"*

Mine has been a life fashioned in the crucible of challenges; the *furnace of affliction*[2]...

A RABBIT TRAIL

Someone said that *life is like a piano. What you get out of it depends on how you play it.* Like Marcus Aurelius, I truly believe that *the art of life is more like wrestling than it is dancing.* The heart and power of a champion is never forged in leisure and comfort; the heart and power of a champion is forged in the raging fires of deep affliction. It is under these conditions that one is tempered.

Without being morbid, the application of high temperatures immediately followed by ice cold ones is rated among the worst torture tactics. The effects on the human body are devastating. For substances such as glass, however, a remarkable thing happens! Tempering, the delicate process of heating and cooling substances, tends to *harden* them! Finding its roots in a Latin word meaning "to season," tempering *seasons* or preserves the glass...

I suppose, writing this, I can see how the *acceptance* of the constant "heating" and "cooling" that life brings can lead to a more seasoned or tempered life. Yet, the price associated with it is often much more than the average person can endure...

The "furnace of affliction" has become my home. Some call this place "The School of Hard Knocks" to signify the lack of ease associated with true, lasting achievement. Whatever it might be called, this is the place I have come to accept as the *rule*, not the *exception*.

Ficus Sycamorus

The sycamore tree is an interesting tree by many standards. Because it was depicted and mentioned in tombs as far back as the Pharaohs, Egypt was called "the land of the Sycamore[1]." Growing up to a height of 150 feet with a 12 foot diameter, this special tree produces timber that is impervious to water. It has an amazing "life expectancy;" some American Sycamores, *Platanus Occidentalis*, were already between 500 and 600 years old by the time the early settlers of America hit the shores of the New World[2]!

All botanical facts aside, the sycamore's inherent zest for life remains intriguing since the tree cannot reproduce by itself. It cannot be reproduced, like most plants, from seeds. The sycamore produces seven crops of fruit each year, remarkably, from small leafless branches. While edible, sycamore fruits do not naturally ripen. To ripen, small wasps lay their eggs in the "eye" of the fruit; "without this, the fruit would not ripen but fall to the ground and rot[3]."

Not only do sycamore fruits *not* ripen naturally, they are naturally bitter. In order for the fruit to be sweetened, it must be *bruised* or incised. The bruising of the fruit introduces air into the fruit that kills the eggs laid by the wasps and causes it to sweeten.

To be clear, when the small wasps lay their eggs in the sycamore fruit, they *cause* it to be bitter *and* prevent seeds from being made. This begins a chain of events that requires that the fruit be *bruised* in order for sweetening to occur...

What has this got to do with you? What has this got to do with beating the odds? Think about it. Could it be that your fruitfulness and ripening is dependent on your sucking it up and taking a little bruising? Remember Marcus Aurelius's thought about life? That it's not a dance but wrestling? Do you think you can honestly get into the ring with Evander Holyfield or Mohammad Ali and not get bruised? Logically, then, there's no way you could get through this thing called *life* and not deal with getting bruised – deal with it!

There's much to be learned from the sycamore. While its wood is impervious to water, its other properties make it hard for woodworkers to craft and its commercial value is diminished[4]. Yet, furniture, tobacco boxes, baskets and veneer are still made from it! Talk about beating the odds! Not only does this tree have unique timber, it is a healing tree. The tree's fruit, sap and bark all have medicinal value. The Egyptians used this property to heal bone fractures, toothaches, inflammations, as well as stomach ailments, to name a few.

I have no idea where you are in your life's timeline. I do know this, though: life's bruising isn't going to get lighter – it's only going to get more *intense*. Unless you get serious about facing reality, you will continue to produce fruit that will be useless – unripe and bitter! That leaves you with only one option: *learn how to endure the bruising required for the ripening of your fruit*. Who knows? Perhaps once you do, your fruit, like that of the sycamore, could be used as a natural sweetener...

Notes

1. Chris Widener, *The Angel Inside: Michelangelo's Secrets for Following Your Passion and Finding the Work You love* (2007)
2. www.kinfonet.org/community/centres/sycamore/tree.html
3. Jane Hill, *American Sycamore: A Hospitable but Somewhat Lonely Tree* (2000). Retrieved from: www.sycamoreisland.org/articles/sa200002.htm
4. www.kinfonet.org/community/centres/sycamore/tree.html
5. Jane Hill, *American Sycamore: A Hospitable but Somewhat Lonely Tree* (2000). Retrieved from: www.sycamoreisland.org/articles/sa200002.htm

3. The Crucible

A strong bull is seen by its scars – Zambian proverb

Sitting on the green and luscious lawn of my Zambian parents' Lusaka West farm, I peered into the distance holding back deep emotions after confessing a slip-up to my good friend, Alex. I am uncertain as to whether the tears that were welling up in my eyes were due to the seething pain of remembering what I had gone through, the relief of confession, the depth of his response, or a combination. Whatever the case may be, what he said to me that warm Zambian day was as significant as it was profound:

> "Kozhi, someday a young person will come to you seeking counsel and guidance. As you speak to this young person, you will look upon your scars and be reminded of how you got to the place where a young person would seek *your* guidance."

I suppose this was Alex's way of telling me that *pain is the crucible in which greatness is forged* and that this would not be the last time I would be experiencing the pain and anguish that comes with discomfort – whether it was my own doing or by the hand of another.

Real generals have *been* on the battlefield…they have *endured* loss…*endured* pain…*endured* the crucible. Their lot is not stars or stripes but scars and pieces of shrapnel. For them, Wheaties® is not their "Breakfast of Champions™;" they endure *pain* for breakfast! You see, "champions are not made in public; they are only recognized there[1]." True champions are made in private…in those cold, damp, and lonely places where only those who *endure* survive. And what is this...cold, damp, and lonely place where champions are forged? *The crucible.*

According to Webster's dictionary, a *crucible* is "a severe test; a place or situation in which concentrated forces interact to cause change or development." Clearly, the crucible is not for everyone. After all, not everyone endures. Think about it: what is *your* "pain threshold?" How much can you *really* take? In other words: what is your breaking point?

In Zambia, we have a simple saying: *Ukutangila te kufika.* Just because one has *begun* does not mean one has *arrived.* Those who *arrive* are those who are *steadfast*...those who have *endured*...those who have *stayed the course.* I shudder to think of how many people stopped just short of arriving. Rather than enduring, they...they gave up.

The word *endure* comes from the French verb *endurer* and means "to (*en*) last (*durer*)[2]." Often, battles and wars are not about who has more firepower but who can last the longest. I am reminded of a scene from the Edward Zwick action film, *The Siege.* In this film, the illegal abduction of a terror suspect by the United States leads to a spite of terrorist bombings in New York City. At the height of public fears and unrest, Annette Bening's character, Elise Kraft (a Middle East CIA expert), leaves to work an informant and says to Denzel Washington's character, Hub: "In this game, the most committed wins." In other words: Those who endure to the end win.

The crucible, according to Webster, is the place where *change* and *development* occur. Not many people can stand the crucible because the price is often *too* high to pay. While the benefits are certainly alluring – wisdom, fame, renown, courage, strength, and many more – the costs are often too steep for many to pay. What price are *you* willing to pay for your destiny? What are you willing to forego for the benefits that come with being pressed on every side?

I did not realize it until later, but Alex was trying to tell me that "*as a result of enduring pain, we change from being mere sufferers to wise counselors and valuable comforters[3].*" There is absolutely *no* shortcut or fast-track to greatness. *"As diamonds are made by pressure and pearls formed by irritation, so greatness is forged by adversity[4]."*

The key to a keen appreciation for challenges, obstacles, and difficulties is *understanding*; understanding the "diamond in the rough." Buried deep within every obstacle, challenge, and difficulty is the prize! Unfortunately,

> Many…face each obstacle in their path with fear and doubt and consider them as enemies when, in truth, these obstructions are friends and helpers. Obstacles are necessary for success because…victory comes only after many struggles and countless defeats. Yet each struggle, each defeat, sharpens your skills and strengths, your courage and your endurance, your ability and your confidence and thus each obstacle is a comrade-in-arms forcing you to become better…or quit. Each rebuff is an opportunity to move forward; turn away from them, avoid them, and you throw away your future[5]

Until we are honest and bold enough – yes, *bold* enough – to *embrace* challenges, difficulties, and obstacles, we willingly enter a never-ending cycle of experiencing the same day…our entire life!

No one…and I mean *no one*…is immune to calamities. Even Biblical Job, who was "blameless and upright, and one who reverently feared God and abstained from and shunned evil[6]", was hit with such calamity that he fell from the penthouse at the Ritz and landed, barely recognizable, at the city dump. Scraping his deformed body with a piece of clay and taking in the foul stench of the city's garbage, with only maggots to keep him company, this "blameless" fellow reminisced being "the greatest of all men of the East[7]."

I suppose he thought about his ten beautiful and successful children, his thriving business enterprise which, in today's terms, would include owning FedEx®, UPS®, the largest trucking and distribution line, a thriving ranching operation, and an unequalled staff and payroll. Blasting back from his past, he realized all of it was *gone*. All of it! Children? *Dead*. Ranch? *Gone*. Staff? *All but four dead*. His health? *Teetering on the brink of death*. Yet this broken soul took on a posture that is foreign to many, if not most, of us. He boldly declares:

> Behold, I go forward, but He is not there. I go backward, but I cannot perceive Him; on the left hand where He works, but I cannot behold Him; He turns Himself to the right hand, but I cannot see Him. But He knows the way that I take. When he has tried me, I shall come forth as refined gold [pure and luminous][8]

In other words, "I don't get it. However, I am going to come out better on the other side." And come out better, he did! The story goes that he rebuilt his business enterprise. Not only so, his *enterprise* became an *empire*! His health? *Restored*. Children? Ten more! This time, his daughters were a combination of Halle Berry, Gisele, and other gorgeous women...all wrapped up in one! The story is that "in all the land there were no women so fair as the daughters of Job[9]."

I know that the skeptic in you is probably saying: "Sure. That is so cliché. 'Coming out better on the other side?' What a load of you know what! My life is not a fairy tale or Biblical story! I have failed, made bad decisions and terrible mistakes...I am in some serious problems and just can't believe there's *even* an *other side*!" Be assured, mon ami(e), that "*even a mistake may turn out to be the one thing necessary to a worthwhile achievement*[10]." Sometimes we need the circumstances and environment to be ripe for change...we need a crucible to be created for our development. The key is for you to learn how to respond to your challenges, difficulties, and obstacles. Zig Ziglar puts it best:

A failure means you've put forth some effort. That's good. Failure gives you an opportunity to learn a better way to do it. That's positive. A failure teaches you something and adds to your experience. That's very helpful. Failure is an event, never a person; an attitude, not an outcome; a temporary inconvenience; a stepping stone. Our response to it determines just how helpful it can be.

Enduring pain is difficult when we feel we are not *responsible* – therefore, *entitled* – to endure such anguish. "Why me?" we ask. "What did I do to *deserve* this?" Perhaps you have lost your job or your mind. Yes, your *mind*. You are at your wits end and the pain is much…too much to bear. Or you have, like Mel Gibson's character in *The Patriot*, lost children and all you can say is: "I have long feared that my sins would return to visit me, and the cost would be more than I could bear." Whatever the circumstance, know that, as the proverb says: *"What can't be cured, must be endured."*

You cannot – no…*must not* – quit! Be like Shakespeare and boldly declare: *"I am tied to the stake, and I must stand the course[11]"* and *"More can I bear than you dare execute[12]."* Remember: *"It is not miserable to be blind; it is miserable to be incapable of enduring blindness[13]."* Take comfort in the knowledge that *"nothing happens to any man that he is not formed by nature to bear[14]."*

Whatever you do, keep your eye on the ball. Do not waver in your endurance. Because,

As in labor, the more one doth exercise, the more one is enabled to do, strength growing upon work; so, with the use of suffering, men's minds get the habit of suffering, and all fears and terrors are to them but as a summons to battle, whereof they know beforehand they shall come off victorious[15]

The "ball" is the impending victory – the crowning, if you will. You cannot and will not get to the crowning unless you endure. So, what's *your* crowning? Is it the doubling of profits in your business? The pay raise you have long-endured for? The home you have saved patiently for? The degree you have sweated years and blood for? Whatever your crowning is, remember:

They attack the one man with their hate and their shower of weapons. But he is like some rock which stretches into the vast sea and which, exposed to the fury of the winds and beaten against by the waves, endures all the violence and threats of heaven and sea, himself standing unmoved[16]

Is that what can be said of you? That even in the face of insurmountable difficulties, violence, tempests, and threats, you have been unmoved?

Notes

1. This quote is attributed to Frankie Mazzapica of Celebration Church
2. *The New Webster Encyclopedic Dictionary of the English Language* (New York: Avenel Books, 1980)
3. Charles R. Swindoll, *Job: A Man of Heroic Endurance* (Nashville, TN: The W Publishing Group, 2004), p.42.
4. Peter Gibbon, *A Call to Heroism*, p.182.
5. Og Mandino, *The Greatest Salesman in the World*, 1968, p.22
6. Job 1:1, Holy Bible, Amplified Version
7. Job 1:3, Holy Bible, Amplified Version

8. Job 23: 8-10, Holy Bible, Amplified Version
9. Job 42:15, Holy Bible, Amplified Version
10. Attributed to Henry Ford
11. William Shakespeare, *King Lear*, Scene III, Act 7
12. William Shakespeare, *King Henry the Fourth*, Part II
13. John Milton, English Poet (1608-1674)
14. Marcus Aurelius (121-180 AD), Roman Emporer, in *Meditations*, Book V, Chapter 18
15. Attributed to Sir Philip Sidney
16. Attributed to Virgil

PART TWO
The BBTO Academy™

Welcome to the BBTO Academy™! The institution of higher learning whose curriculum is not penned by human hands and whose philosophies are not contemplated by mortal minds. The BBTO Academy™ is a place where, within your first few days, you'll learn, in Forrest Gump's words, that *"it"* happens. It is a place where there is no control. It is a place where hurricanes, tornadoes, floods, and earthquakes all meet and shake the very foundations of what we believe to be true or false, fair or unfair, right or wrong.

The word academy is derived from the Latin and Greek words *academia* and *acadēmeia*. The word was made "famous" because the land upon which Plato built his Academy originally belonged to the Greek hero, *Acadēmus*. In the strictest sense, an academy is a school or college of special training and also represents an association established for the promotion of literature, the arts, and sciences. All things being equal, an academy is where refinement *can* and *should* occur…

The BBTO Academy™ is such a place: one where refinement is the *modus operandi*. It is the crucible (ah…there's that word again) in which concentrated forces meet to either *forge* us or *break* us. The Germans have a saying that the same hammer can perform two functions: *forge steel* or *shatter glass*. The BBTO Academy™ is where we learn what we're really made of. It is in this Academy that we discover our Achilles Heel and whether or not we are willing to overcome it.

The BBTO Academy™ is where we develop an attitude about who we are and want to be. I constantly remind my Interpersonal Communication students that an attitude is a *learned* predisposition to *respond* to anything in a favorable or unfavorable way. So, to you I say, the Academy is the place where we learn about responses. It is where we learn just how quickly we can think on our feet…

4. Disappointments

Unhappiness is best defined as the difference between our talents and our expectations[1]

Disappointment has many faces; probably as many as there are people! Its root word, disappoint, is derived from the French word *désappointer* which means to *remove from an appointment or office*. It is akin to one being given the Vice Presidency of a certain region and then being removed. What was an *appointment* – to the office of Vice President – is now a *dis*appointment.

In modern English, however, disappointment is connotative with a strong *emotion* that we feel when our desires – expected or not – have not been met[2]. Because it is an emotion, disappointment can be so rough that some definitions go so far as to classify it as a "mental upset[3]." Disappointment often breeds feelings of failure, defeat, and frustration. When *a* disappointment becomes a *series* of *disappointments*, the effects on the mind and heart can be quite devastating…

Consider a young boy who looks forward to nothing more than playing catch with his father. The first time his father does not make it, the young boy's disappointment is evident in the fact that he could not just be with his daddy. Subsequent disappointments – especially related to not making it – then lead to more complex issues such as a lack of trust. These, in turn, lead to even more difficult social and developmental issues in the boy's life.

This example notwithstanding, it is undeniable that life is filled with disappointments. Whether we set our expectations on something or not, the simple fact that we do not always get what we desire creates potent circumstances for us to get disappointed. It is a fact of life that we will be disappointed; by our friends, our family, strangers, the weather…and many more.

The BBTO Academy™ includes, in its curriculum, a "class" in Disappointments. The reason? It is a simple fact of life: *we will be disappointed*. No matter our color, creed, upbringing, or circumstances, we will have to *endure* disappointments. The British Poet, Alexander Pope noted: *'Blessed is the man who expects nothing, for he shall never be disappointed'* was the ninth beatitude. The *only* way that you will not have to endure disappointments is to not expect anything at all. Realistically, this is impossible; *none* of us are immune to disappointments.

Learning to deal with – and appreciate – disappointments is part of the core curriculum in the BBTO Academy™ precisely because there is no escaping it. Did you know that beating the odds is facilitated by disappointments? You see, *if you will be quiet and ready enough, you will find compensation in every disappointment*[4]! Seriously, one of the odds you get to beat is refusing to be defeated by setbacks and disappointments…

While I advocate for an appreciation for disappointments, I have to honestly say that, even with the knowledge of "compensation in every disappointment," it is bittersweet. Consider that…

> …in 1858, the Illinois legislature elected Stephen A. Douglas senator instead of Abraham Lincoln. A sympathetic friend asked Lincoln how he felt. "Like the boy who stubbed his toe; I am too big to cry and too badly hurt to laugh[5]."

While Lincoln eventually overcame and accomplished much, it is clear from these words that dealing with disappointment is not for the fainthearted. The pain and anguish associated with disappointment causes *dissonance* that can be much to handle.

Yet, and even so, the BBTO Academy™ pushes this curriculum on us because there is no shortcut or end-run to the summit; at least not without facing disappointment head on. There is no graduation, no victory, without going through this class and passing it.

Notes

1. Edward de Bono, British Physician and Writer
2. See Wikipedia
3. See Dictionary.com
4. Henry David Thoreau
5. Clifton Fadiman & André Bernard. *Bartlett's Book of Anecdotes*, 2000, Little, Brown and Company.

5. Betrayals

Just for a handful of silver he left us, just for a riband to stick in his coat[1]

Much like disappointment, betrayal takes on many faces. Sometimes, it shows its ugly face when a secret is revealed. Other times, it burrows out of the earth when loyalty turns to disloyalty or when one is treacherously delivered and exposed to one's enemies. Whichever face betrayal takes, the effect is the same – we are deeply hurt.

My favorite of Shakespeare's tragedies is *Othello: The Moor of Venice*. It has all the ingredients for a typical Shakespearean Tragedy...and more. The relationships, manipulation, and betrayal make for such dramatic reading, one might feel as though one was reading something that happened in our time. Sadly, Iago's betrayal in this tragedy is not fictional; few of us get to celebrate our twelfth birthday without having been betrayed. While the intensity of the betrayal is different for us all, betrayal can spark some very negative feelings in us. These feelings can be so negative, they can douse the BBTO Spirit™ in us.

Betrayal, just like disappointment, is something that we cannot hide from. The only reasonable way to avoid it is to not get close to anyone – no friends, no family, no spouse...nothing. As long as you and I get close to people, the chances of getting betrayed increase. The BBTO Academy™ has Betrayals in its core curriculum simply because we cannot avoid it. Without an understanding of betrayal, the BBTO Spirit™ continues to be dormant in us...

Part of growing and appreciating the role that betrayal plays in our lives is us being *realistic*. According to Philip K. Dick, *reality is that which, when you stop believing in it, doesn't go away*. *No one* is immune to betrayal! Othello was betrayed by Iago...Julius Caesar was betrayed by Marcus Junius

49

Brutus...even Jesus was betrayed by Judas. While Othello is a fictional character, all the above were highly successful in their chosen pursuits. Who are we to think we could possibly find success without enduring betrayal? Ralph Waldo Emerson's characteristic definition of success includes the ability to endure betrayal:

> To laugh often and much; to win the respect of intelligent people and the affection of children; to earn the approbation of honest critics and *endure the betrayal of false friends*; to appreciate beauty; to find the best in others; to give of one's self; to leave the world a bit better, whether by a healthy child, a garden patch, or a redeemed social condition; to have played and laughed with enthusiasm and sung with exultation; to know even one life has breathed easier because you have lived - this is to have succeeded.

If we are to develop the BBTO Spirit™, we must be willing to accept the fact that betrayal is a natural progression for successful people. Not only is betrayal a natural hurdle on the way to the finish line, it makes us unique "athletes." You see, hurdlers are unlike any other track athletes. Not only are they required to have forward motion; they are also required to have upward motion...

Notes

1. Robert Browning (1812-1889), British Poet. *The Lost Leader*
2. Clifton Fadiman & André Bernard. *Bartlett's Book of Anecdotes*, 2000, Little, Brown and Company.

6. Rejections

Dear to us are those who love us...but dearer are those who reject us as unworthy, for they add another life; they build a heaven before us whereof we had not dreamed, and thereby supply to us new powers out of the recesses of the spirit, and urge us to new and unattempted performances[1]

The Latin word *réjectus* is where the root word of rejection (reject) is derived. It simply means *to throw back*. If you are reading this book and have not yet experienced rejection, wait a *little* while longer! Rejection is the lot of those with a BBTO Spirit™. Their ideas, thoughts, plans, feelings, love, etc, is thrown back – *very often*. Most of the most successful people in various fields of endeavor have experienced and endured rejection...

> At a reception, Beethoven, who was then still known only as a pianist, mentioned his desire to have an arrangement with a publisher similar to that enjoyed by Goethe and Handel. That is, anything he wrote would belong to the publisher in perpetuity in return for a guaranteed lifetime income. "My dear young man, you must not complain," sneered his interlocutor, "for you are neither a Goethe nor a Handel, and it is not to be expected that you will ever be, for such masters will not be born again[2]."

Ludwig van Beethoven (1770-1827), who was instrumental in transitioning Western Classical Music from the Classical to the Romantic eras, is now among the most famous, influential, and beloved composers of *all time*. What is little known about Beethoven is that he started going deaf at the age of twenty yet continued to compose and conduct great music. For him to do that, however, he had to deal with and endure rejection...

In order for us to have the correct posture for the BBTO Academy™, we need to *toughen* up! There is a story that Diogenes, the Greek philosopher who lived between 412 and 323 BC, was once seen begging from a statue. When asked why he was involved in such a futile exercise, he replied: "*I am exercising the art of being rejected*[3]!"

Yes! Go to those extremes, if you must. But you cannot allow yourself to let rejection be the end of your quest. Rejection is not limited to you, and you alone. We have all been rejected, to some degree. That pretty girl in fifth grade that wouldn't have anything to do with you – she rejected you. That proposal that you worked overtime to increase efficiency on a project – the boss rejected it (and, in your eyes, rejected *you*). The bank that wouldn't give you that loan – they rejected you. So what?!!

Get off your high horse! What makes you think you should not experience rejection? Does this world owe you a thing? Does the bank? The credit card company? The boss? That boy or girl who rejected you in fifth grade? None of these people or institutions owe you a thing! Learn from Diogenes; get used to being rejected – it will happen again and again and again. Learn to *embrace* rejection! Great feats are borne in the aftermath of rejection. Great works of art and literature have been crafted out of the ashes of burned hopes. It is *not* over even though the fat lady has *already* sung! There's always another show!

Wallowing is not going to make things better. All that wallowing does is help us dig ourselves deeper into a hole. Remember: the first rule of holes...*stop digging*! We all experience rejection – it must be an expected part of life. I was always shy and would not approach girls...until I was told, "What's the worst that can happen? That she says 'no'?" Those words changed my perspective. So...what's the worst that can happen? That someone says "no?"

My self-worth is not dependent on who accepts or rejects me. *No one* will *ever* determine my value – that is, no one but *me*. I am not trying to minimize the emotion we feel when we have been rejected. It throws us out of whack – especially the more esteem we give whatever it is we were pursuing. *Fine.* Go ahead and feel the crushing associated with rejection. But, please, don't let that quench the fire of the BBTO Spirit™ in you! We cannot give up, give in, or give out. Those of us seeking to refine or rekindle the BBTO Spirit™ have a simple motto. When faced with insurmountable difficulties and odds, we boldly declare:

> *We keep going back, stronger, not weaker, because we will not allow rejection to beat us down. It will only strengthen our resolve. To be successful, there is no other way[4].*

Indeed, there is *no* other way! We are "in spite of" people – we "BBTOers™." We recognize that life isn't fair. We know that we are not going to have things go our way. We know that we are not fully equipped to handle a lot of things. We know that we may not have the education, pedigree or wherewithal to do a lot of things. Yet, *in spite of* these impediments, we wear our gloves each day and go twelve rounds with life. We get out of the ring after rejection's right hook has dealt its full blow exhausted, bruised, battered, and broken but resolve to heal and return for more the next day. "Perhaps tomorrow I'll get a few more licks in," we say to ourselves...

Notes

1. Ralph Waldo Emerson (1803-1882), American philosopher, clergyman, and orator
2. Clifton Fadiman & André Bernard. *Bartlett's Book of Anecdotes*, 2000, Little, Brown and Company.
3. *Ibid*
4. Earl G. Graves, Sr. (1935 -), author, publisher, entrepreneur, and philanthropist. Founder of Black Enterprise Magazine

7. Losses

All I know from my own experience is that the more loss we feel, the more grateful we should be for whatever it was we had to lose. It means that we had something worth grieving for. The ones I'm sorry for are the ones that go through life not knowing what grief is[1]

Those with the BBTO Spirit™ are more than *cognizant* of loss; like Christ, they are "acquainted with grief[2]." They understand that *"what has been lost was never possible to keep in the first place[3]."* They know what it feels like to be deprived or dispossessed of things of value.

I have lost many things over the years. The impact each loss has had on me has been both trivial and significant. Some things I have lost and simply forgotten that I lost them. Others, yet, have been lost and there is no forgetting them. The loss has been etched on the walls of both my mind and my heart. Usually, the BBTO Spirit™ is either *spurred* by loss or *snuffed* by it. In the last few years, mine has been spurred…but the cost has been dear. Loss did not come with any subtlety, by the way; when it rained on me, it poured and cut through to my very core…

Life's nature dictates that the experience of loss isn't like Chicken Pox; just because you've had it once doesn't mean you're immune to it and won't get it again. Because life is a cycle, we will lose loved ones as they "rotate" through the cycle…we will lose jobs as companies fold, are acquired, or become more lean…we will lose possessions as our homes and vehicles are broken into…we will lose our sense of direction as our thoughts turn from fruitfulness to poverty and lack…we *will* lose…

We begin to minimize the impact of loss as we recognize that it is a part of life's cycle. When we accept that what we have lost has a specific purpose in our growth process, the BBTO Academy™ is increasing in value. I know that this might sound like a rationalization of terrible events but it is not; this is "Larger Purpose Thinking™." We have to see beyond isolated incidences and events. We have to ask ourselves:

- What's really going on here?
- What am I supposed to learn from this situation?
- How does this situation play into the larger picture of my life?
- How am I to respond to this situation?
- Why is the timing of this incidence or event significant?
- Why were the circumstances and I brought together?

Each incident and event in our lives plays a larger role in shaping our character and future. We miss it when we allow the pain associated with the loss we have experienced to cloud our "Larger Purpose Thinking™." There is *nothing* pleasant about losing things and people we value. Yet, there is a lesson to be learned from this loss. We learn what is *truly* valuable to us.

This process of learning what is valuable to us requires "recycling" since man is prone to complacency. We often don't know how much we value something until it is not within reach – when we have lost it to eternity (death) or to those who would rob us. Without "Larger Purpose Thinking™," we are faced with *despair without payoff*. I don't know about you but I live life knowing that there is reciprocation; my sorrow will be turned to joy, my hunger to fullness, and my weakness to strength. If I am going to despair, let it be a seed that will produce valuable fruit in my near future. If I don't think about the larger picture when faced with loss, I am scattering my seeds on the pavement where they *will* sprout but will not thrive and produce fruit for *anyone*.

Dr. Kozhi Sidney Makai

The antonym of loss is gain. Without "Larger Purpose Thinking™," it is easy for us to fail to see that there is gain in some of our losses. You see, *there are occasions when it is undoubtedly better to incur loss than to make gain*[4]. For instance, in the United States, section 165 of the Internal Revenue Code provides that economic losses may be deducted from adjusted gross income. This means that one would be liable for less tax (gain). As a growing boy, my mother always told me, "When one door is closed (loss), another one has been opened (gain)." This "balance" of life is something that she continues to tell me. Loss is never the end of a thing...

I'd be wrong to claim that I am "ok" with loss; definitely not! There are a lot of things and people that I wish I did not lose. Yet, "Larger Purpose Thinking™" reminds me that each loss facilitates gains. In other words, unless I lose some things, I cannot gain others. Had I been holding on to some of the things and people I had in the past, I may not have what I have now. There are friends that I have lost that became the impetus for me gaining other friends. Had I held on to those friends, it is quite possible that I would not have the friends I currently have.

It is worth mentioning that the "fear of loss" rates among the worst of self-destructive mindsets. When we fear loss, we try to hold tightly to those things we *believe* are the most valuable to us. We throw "Larger Purpose Thinking™" out of the window and fail to see people and things going through the "recycling" process of life. When people hoard money, they tend to lose it. When parents hold on too tightly to their children, like wet soap, they jump out of their hands. When one holds on jealously to a significant other, their obsessive and possessive nature pushes the person out of their lives. The fear of loss is dangerous because *we attract what we fear*[5].

Instead of being fearful, we must have faith that there is a larger purpose being fulfilled. Rather than lament what we have lost, we must remember: *Wise men never sit and wail their loss, but cheerily seek how to redress their harms*[6]. There's

56

something greater at play – and, usually, it is for our own good.

Sadly, we are extremely *selfish* as we lament losses. Think about it. What were your thoughts when you lost a loved one? How many times did you put the words "I" and "me" in your laments? Get it now? We've got to get away from this selfish posture and recognize our losses for what they *really* are: preambles and introductions to a *new* and *exciting* chapter in our lives...

Notes

1. Frank O'Connor (1903-1966), Irish Author and Political Activist
2. Isaiah 53:3. Holy Bible, King James Version.
3. Laura Teresa Marquez, *Early Morning Conversation*
4. Titus Maccius Plautus (born 254 BC), Roman playwright
5. Florence Scovel Shinn (1871-1940), *The Game of Life and How to Play it*
6. William Shakespeare

8. Jealousy

It is not love that is blind, but jealousy[1]

Another crucial ingredient to the crucible in which the BBTO Spirit™ is developed is jealousy. While our own jealousies will impede our development and growth, nothing can *potentially* do us in more than the jealousies of others. When others are jealous, they are resentful of our successes or advantages.

Quel Catastrophe![2]

In 1962, the Irish novelist, playwright, and poet Samuel Beckett (1906-1989) married his longtime companion, Suzanne. Soon afterward, their relationship was marred by her jealousy of his fame and success as a writer. One day in 1969, the phone rang. After listening for a moment, she spoke briefly to the caller and hung up. Motivated by jealousy and green with envy, she turned to Beckett and whispered, "*Quel catastrophe!*" This is French for "What a catastrophe!" Apparently, she had just been informed that Beckett had been awarded the Nobel Prize for Literature by the Swedish Academy.

People who are jealous are often very close to us. They are those whom we respect and hold in high regard. As in Beckett's case, often times, it is family members and those in our closest confidence that end up being most jealous of us! The American comedian and actor Rodney Dangerfield (1921-2004) quipped at the sad nature of jealousy: *My wife's jealousy is getting ridiculous. The other day she looked at my calendar and wanted to know who May was!*

Those who are jealous, however, are not limited to those closest to us. At a banquet given by the grand cardinal of Spain, Columbus was seated at the most honored place and served with great deference and ceremony. A courtier, jealous of the foreigner's success, asked him rudely whether he thought that if he had not discovered the New World somebody else would have done so. Columbus did not reply at once, but, taking an egg in his hand, invited the guest to make it stand on one end. All tried and failed, whereupon Columbus cracked the egg against the table in such a way as to flatten one end. Then he set it standing on the crushed part. The moral was plain to the company: once he had shown the way, anyone could follow it.[3]

Jealousy is completely blind; it knows no names. Whether you are doing well or doing poorly, people will be jealous. You see, *the jealous are possessed by a mad devil and a dull spirit at the same time*[4]. They cannot see the death they bring to their own souls since *jealousy is the jaundice of the soul*[5]. It distorts and discolors one's better judgment such that things are said and done that may not otherwise be said or done…

Rest assured, however, that *there is never jealousy where there is not strong regard*[6]. Those who are jealous have seen something in us worth envying. You can take this however you wish but, if you were to see this as a positive thing, you would not be deterred from your goals or vision. You would, instead, use *their* jealousy as a *prop* for *your* stage! Success's costs come at a very high price; you may not be hounded by the paparazzi but you will be hounded by jealous friends, family, and strangers. The only way to possibly (again, *possibly*) avoid this is to remain mediocre and not reach out for more…

But what would that do to enhance the world? What value does the world gain from your hidden talent? What legacy would be left to your name if you caved in? The Gospels paint an interesting picture of the Pharisees and Sadducees; they were green with envy! Their fight with Jesus was *personal*; it had little to do with doctrine. Call it human nature, if you must; people just have an uncanny predilection for jealousy. Jesus' own disciple's fought amongst themselves; trying to figure out who would sit at His right hand and be the big cheese...

I know...it is a hard thing to admit: jealous streaks are simply a large part of human nature. Take a child, for example: everything is fine until *another* child begins to play with a toy the child was *not* playing with or the attention shifts from the child to *another* child. I can't say with certainty that we are born with jealousy; but, this character flaw can be overcome (both personally and that which is directed towards us). And, to be perfectly honest, we have *no* choice but to overcome it.

For now, suffice it to say that another person's jealousy is simply not enough to deter me from becoming who I was destined to be. Another person's jealousy lacks the power to snuff out the BBTO Spirit™ in me – that is, unless I give it power. Let us, therefore, accept the fact that jealousies exist; but let us give them no power. Let us plough through them and know that, like negative thoughts, they gain power from our meditating upon them. Rather than give them power, let us strip them of their power by advancing towards that which we know to be our truest passions and desires...daily...

Notes

1. Lawrence George Durrell (1912-1990), British Novelist, Poet, Dramatist and Travel Writer
2. Clifton Fadiman & André Bernard. *Bartlett's Book of Anecdotes*, 2000, Little, Brown and Company.
3. *Ibid*
4. Johann Kasper Lavater (1741-1801), Swiss poet and physiognomist
5. John Dryden (1631-1700), English poet, playwright, and dramatist
6. Washington Irving (1783-1859), American writer known for creating the character Rip Van Winkle.

9. Discouragements

Every great work, every great accomplishment, has been brought into manifestation through holding to the vision, and often just before the big achievement, comes apparent failure and discouragement[1]

Discouragement is a plague upon the soul. No matter how hard you fight it, it finds a way in. For the achiever, discouragement is what kryptonite is to Superman®...the ultimate killer. When we are discouraged, we have literally been *stripped of courage*...we have *lost heart* (disheartened)...we have been *deprived of self-confidence and hope*. BBTOers™ thrive on having courage, self-confidence, and hope; without these, the entire premise behind the BBTO Spirit™ is brought to naught...

Institutionalized?

One of my favorite drama movies is *The Shawshank Redemption*. Starring Tim Robbins and Morgan Freeman, it follows the dramatic experiences of a young banker's wrongful life imprisonment and the ensuing development of a bond of friendship between the two leading characters. Red (Freeman), who believes that when a man has been long confined to the walls of a cell and the "rules" of prison, he becomes *institutionalized* – he cannot function on the "outside." I suppose it is this view that leads him to angrily tell Andy (Robbins) that "on the inside, hope can get a man killed."

What Red did not understand is that hope is what keeps us *alive*! Discouragement – the *loss of hope* – then, is akin to being *choked*...snuffing out life. It can quite easily take everything out of us. Even so, we have no choice but to rise above it – no matter what it takes! You see, *discouragement and failure are two of the surest stepping stones to success*[3]. We are all going to experience discouragement. Even the great American evangelist Billy Graham confessed: *The Christian life is not a constant high. I have my moments of deep discouragement. I have to go to God in prayer with tears in my eyes, and say, 'O God, forgive me," or "Help me."*

Refuse to be institutionalized! Refuse to accept discouragement – *a lack of hope* – as a way of life. Rise up! Take on the attitude of Vincent Van Gogh who said: *In spite of everything I shall rise again: I will take up my pencil, which I have forsaken in my great discouragement, and I will go on with my drawing.* Pick the pieces up and do your best with what's left. All is not lost – not until *you* decide it is.

I know…discouragement can make us feel inadequate, like we simply don't measure up. Remember, though: *Discouragement is not the absence of adequacy but the absence of courage*[4]. You may have lost your courage but that doesn't mean you are not adequate to the task or dream. Though discouraged, we have to fight and press on. *What we do not see, what most of us never suspect of existing, is the silent but irresistible power which comes to the rescue of those who fight on in the face of discouragement*[5]. Think about it: *Permanence, perseverance and persistence in spite of all obstacles, discouragement, and impossibilities; it is this, that in all things distinguishes the strong soul from the weak*[6].

We have to press on no matter how overwhelming the odds are. *The most essential factor is persistence - the determination never to allow your energy or enthusiasm to be dampened by the discouragement that must inevitably come*[7]. Discouragement is inevitable. We *will* be defeated. We are not going to win every battle. Yet, *defeat should never be a source of discouragement but rather a fresh stimulus*[8].

Notes

1. Florence Scovel Shinn (1871-1940), American author, philosopher and spiritual leader

2. *The New Webster Encyclopedic Dictionary of the English Language* (New York: Avenel Books, 1980)
3. Dale Carnegie (1888-1955), American lecturer and author
4. Anonymous
5. Napoleon Hill (1883-1970), American author
6. Thomas Carlyle (1795-1881), a leading figure in the Victorian era, he was a Scottish historian and essayist
7. James Whitcomb Riley (1849-1916), American writer and poet
8. Robert South (1634-1716), English churchman

PART THREE
Nurturing the BBTO Spirit™

Everything in Part II "happens" to us; whether we like it or not, what "happens" to us is the Academy in which the BBTO Spirit™ is developed. What we do with what "happens" to us is a personal choice; while we may not be able to choose the circumstances, we are responsible for our reactions to these circumstances. But, to be clear, there is nothing we can do about that which happens to us – *nothing*. We can no more influence what happens than we can the rising or the setting of the sun…

This is not to say that we are "hopeless" in this situation. As I have illustrated, there is *something* that can be done. However, what can be done has *nothing* to do with the circumstances themselves. All we can do is be "reactive" and, sometimes, be preemptive by preparing for such situations. But even with the most astute preparation, sometimes all we can do is react…

In this part of the book, we will look at how we can be "effectively preemptive" in nurturing the BBTO Spirit™. We will look at three basic ideals that will help us hone our BBTO Spirit™ for maximum exploitation. These three traits allow us to play a more *active* role in developing the spirit that can change the landscape of our lives…

10. Improvise

If there is a trait which does characterize leaders it is opportunism. Successful people are very often those who steadfastly refuse to be daunted by disadvantage and have the ability to turn disadvantage to good effect. They are people who seize opportunity and take risks[1]

One of my all-time favorite television shows is *MacGyver*. The show, whose main tagline was "His mind is the ultimate weapon[1]", was on air for seven seasons (1985-1992). Other taglines[2] for the show were:

"For him, saving the day is all in a day's work."
"The right man when things go wrong."
"He acts fast and thinks faster."
"Part boy-scout. Part genius. All hero."
"Always prepared for adventure."

What is great about Richard Dean Anderson's character, MacGyver, is that he never uses a gun on his missions; *just his brain*. He epitomizes the American Heritage Dictionary's definition of improvise by making do with available materials.

No matter the situation, MacGyver always *finds a way*. Because he improvises with the most common material, there is no science fiction to it. He uses materials that *would* normally be in a particular area or situation. To me, the lesson is simple: if MacGyver can do it, so can we…

In Zambia, such a disposition, the ability to improvise, is referred to as being "a MacGyver." And, growing up, I learned early that life *rarely* provides all that we need for our cocktails. I am certain you've heard that when you've got lemons, you can make lemonade, right? If you routinely follow this logic, you are free to call yourself a MacGyver – one who always *seems* to be prepared for the adventure.

You may not have all that you need for your particular endeavor; however, that does not get you off the hook. You are still liable for accomplishing your endeavor. You must *improvise* and make do with what you *do* have. Remember that life owes you *nothing*; all that's available is for the taking and you must take some initiative.

Turn Things Up!

If there's anything to be learned from my personal experience thus far, it is that we need to *have* and *take* initiative. There is *no* "perfect aligning of the stars." While some doors will be opened for you, others you must break down! Garfield said: *Things don't turn up in this world until somebody turns them up.* Turn things up! Initiative is "one's personal, responsible decision[3]." It is "the first *active* procedure in any enterprise[4]" (emphasis mine). Without it, we merely exist. There is no *fullness* to our existence and no *life* to our being.

Sometimes our ship won't come in; we have to swim to it! The English have a proverb that articulates the need for initiative well: *Do not lie in a ditch, and say God help me; use the lawful tools He hath lent thee.* If opportunity doesn't knock – build a door[5]! Don't make any excuses; take some initiative. You see, *things may come to those who wait, but only things left by those who hustle[6]*. You have to decide just how badly you desire what you seek. You might be going through something right now that makes you feel like you just can't catch a break. You feel like there's simply no opportunity in your radius of reach. Alright, then; make one! After all, *a wise man will make more opportunities than he finds[8]*. This is how it works: *Vigilance in watching opportunity; tact and daring in seizing upon opportunity; force and persistence in crowding opportunity to its utmost of possible achievement – these are the martial virtues which must command success[9]*.

Dr. Kozhi Sidney Makai

A Butter Knife

Beating the odds has a lot to do with the options we have and the choices we make. Before you dismiss this as being cliché, please hear me out. Every now and then, we are faced with situations where our options are completely limited – there's simply *little* we can do. We are out of options and, if we are to make it (define "make it" however you will), we have to improvise. Improvising is a *choice*; one that we make depending on how badly we desire something...

Growing up in Zambia, I was thrust into a world where improvising was the norm, not the exception. Thank God for power tools! But I used my first power tool here in the United States working construction. Before that, it was all manual and, even so, there was a lot of improvising involved.

For instance, post-hole diggers were my first "aha" tool. They were an "aha" tool because instead of having one flat side, it has two and they form a center that actually pulls the dirt out of the hole. Back in Zambia, as my father, my brothers, and I built cow fences, we did not have post-hole diggers. We had one six-foot piece of iron that we flattened at the end and used to dig our holes. As we dug, we would have to stop several times to remove the dirt from the hole using our bare hands. The lack of "proper" tools did not deter us from making the necessary holes. What drove us was simple: *It had to be done.*

I was the family "fix it all" growing up. My parents, from their somewhat British upbringing, would say I was a "Jack of all trades and master of none." Whatever! If the stereo quit working, I would fix it. If the lights were acting up, I was an electrician and fixed the problem. Irrigation piping? Handled that too. As a matter of fact, my mother loves to tell the story of my older brothers and father failing to figure out the correct configuration of a brand new piping system we had just acquired. I remember that vaguely but my mother says I walked up, took one look at it all, and said,

"No, this piece goes here." With that, the entire system was connected correctly.

Interestingly, most times, I did not have the correct tools for most of my jobs. For instance, when a flathead screwdriver was not available, I discovered that a butter knife is a perfect *substitute*. I believe certain old habits die hard because I just looked at my tool box recently and guess what I have in there? A butter knife!

What's *your* butter knife? What is it that could use some improvising in your world? Are you too busy complaining about the fact that you do not have the right tools? If you are, you are not ready to face your true destiny – you don't want it *badly* enough. *If necessity is the mother of all invention, then improvising is the mother of accomplishment.* Without it, nothing will get done...

Anyone that has taken an ethics course will know that there are very few, if any, absolutes in life. We deal with so much gray area that we have to think quickly on our feet. Often, there is rarely time to think – just act. This means that we have to improvise and "make do" with whatever is available. We each have to find our butter knife...

It's Not the Hand that Matters

I recently began playing Poker; thanks to my American brother, Kelly. *Who wouldn't, if someone else was buying you in*?! Anyway, if there is one thing that we have no control over, it is what cards we're going to be dealt. It's all *probability*. Dictionary.com defines probability as:

(a) The relative possibility that an event will occur, as expressed by the ratio of the number of actual occurrences to the total number of possible occurrences.
(b) The relative frequency with which an event occurs or it likely to occur.

Because there are a certain number of cards in each deck of cards, I have a one in four chance of being dealt an Ace, two through ten, a Jack, Queen, or King. Even for those that count cards when they play, they have no idea what they will be dealt as each hand is begun. Sometimes, you are dealt "pocket Aces" and other times you are dealt cards that make you want to throw something. What is most important, however, isn't which cards you have been dealt; it is *how you play them.*

Sometimes, your "pocket Aces" may be a natural gifting and endowment of athletic or critical thinking ability (or whatever other valuable gifting). Either way, your "pocket Aces" mean little if you are not willing to improvise and make do with what you have. If you don't believe me, visit some of the basketball playgrounds of New York, Indiana, or Houston and you'll find many people who were dealt "pocket Aces" but failed to capitalize on them. They have a plethora of excuses about why they failed to make an "Exploitation Opportunity™" out of it.

I did not know that I had a valuable basketball skill and ability. When I was growing up, basketball was not a sport kids played until they reached eighth grade. By the time I was in fifth or sixth grade, however, my brothers, who were in high school, played during school holidays. I used to watch them and learn from them and their friends. Rather than wait until eighth grade, I decided to improvise and get a head start on the game. I became a *student* of the game…

Almost through my entire career, I did not have the best attire for basketball; not the shoes, the shorts, or the shirts. I remember playing with such worn out shoes once, the sole of the shoes had holes that exposed my socks (whatever was left of them) and feet to the tarred practice and game floors. To this day, I have calluses on the inside part of my feet from that experience. What a friend calls my battle scars…

However, I knew that basketball was my "pocket Aces." It was the one thing that I could do well and I could thrive at doing. So I kept a supply of insoles (how I wish Dr.

Scholl's® had made his *"gellin'"* insoles then!) and cardboard to keep my feet from hurting too much. I mean, what else could I do? Figure that the lack of proper equipment was reason enough for me to give it all up?

Life deals us some really tough breaks – *a lot.* Some things just knock the wind out of us. We're knocked to the ground with such force that we are left shocked and hurting. While some people choose to "stay down," others, those with the BBTO Spirit™, *get up* and refuse to be *done like that.* It is not the hand that matters; it's how you play it. With a little improvising, you could easily *bluff* for the whole pot!

Notes

1. John Viney, *Drive* (London: Bloomsbury Publishing PLC, 1999)
2. *MacGyver on* www.imdb.com/title/tt0088559/
3. *Ibid*
4. Initiative. Dictionary.com
5. *The New Webster Encyclopedic Dictionary of the English Language* (New York: Avenel Books, 1980)
6. Attributed to Milton Berle (1908-2002), the Emmy-winning American comedian
7. Attributed to Abraham Lincoln (1809-1865), sixteenth President of the United States
8. Francis Bacon (1561-1626), English philosopher, statesman, and essayist credited for creating the English essay
9. Austin Phelps (1820-1890), American minister and educator

11. Overcome

Overcome, o-ver-kum. To conquer; to vanquish; to surmount; to get the better of; to gain the superiority; to be victorious[1]

No *one* runs the race to get second place. Every person in the race is after *one* thing – *first* place. Each contender seeks to *prevail* against the others to emerge the winner. That sperm that is now about half of you gained superiority, surmounted and conquered serious odds, got the better of and vanquished the others to emerge victorious. In short, it *overcame*. The same BBTO Spirit™ that drove that sperm to perform this insurmountable task lives in you. It may be active, it may be dormant; but it's *in* you!

Nurturing the BBTO Spirit™ requires a serious reorientation towards what it means to fight. Fortunately for you and I, "*the race is not to the swift nor the battle to the strong, neither is bread to the wise nor riches to men of intelligence and understanding nor favor to men of skill[2].*" A modern translation of this is:

> The fastest runner doesn't always win the race, and the strongest warrior doesn't always win the battle. The wise are often poor, and the skillful are not necessarily wealthy. And those who are educated don't always lead successful lives[3].

This means that we have a *fighting* chance...

The Wussification of America[4]

Sitting at the table playing a board game with my friend and her seven-year old daughter, I experienced something that is now rare. When my friend's daughter wanted to replay a turn, her mother would *not* have it (reminded me of the "loving" nature of giraffes). No matter how much her daughter pouted, she was unmoved. This scene was picturesque: a *real* mother teaching a lesson that would, someday, save the *life* of her child. When I reminded her of the scene a few days later, she said, "Kozhi, she has to learn two things: first, you don't always win; second, there's always a winner and a loser."

My friend often does not take my parenting compliments seriously; she often feels like she is not doing enough. However, I honestly believe that she is giving her daughter the best gift – *the development of an overcoming spirit.* The world is not getting safer; there isn't a single continent at present not dealing with conflict. The world is only going to get more and more complicated. My friend is developing her daughter so that she will effectively face whatever challenges come her way.

Conversely, I am not sure if you have noticed but we are breeding a generation without backbone (a bunch of wusses). The scene above is becoming rarer and rarer. We refuse to make *overcomers* out of our children by wiping their noses and coddling them through life. And, to be perfectly honest, we'd be hypocritical if we tried to teach them to be overcomers, wouldn't we? How can we teach them to be overcomers when *we* don't understand what it means to be an overcomer? When we expect life to be a walk in the park? Or when we crawl into a corner immediately there's no wind in our sails or a little tempest hits our ships? Consider a couple of examples of today's social development:

1. Teachers in some school districts can no longer grade assignments in red ink (it "hurts" the kids' "self-esteem").
2. In sports, "everyone is a winner" and "everyone gets a trophy."

I am *not* an advocate of making three year olds fight to the bitter end in a soccer game but I am an advocate of them understanding that some people *win* and others *lose*. If we create the illusion that they are doing great when they are not, we are setting them on a slippery slope that *will* eventually affect their self-esteem. Anything short of the truth creates an expectation of being owed something; an entitlement attitude.

If we are to someday pass the reins on to a *responsible* generation, we must first make sure that we are *realistic* in our *expectations* and *development* of the generation. As a society, the pendulum swings from one *extreme* to another instead of finding a reasonable medium. If we are not expecting our children to perform miracles, we are developing them to never work hard for anything. Put together, we have a generation that will be ill-prepared for the rigors of the challenges to follow in the coming generations. Why? Simply put: because they are accustomed to having it easy. They are accustomed to automation and having *someone else* fix things for them...

This book is not a treatise on parenting or social development. The preceding portion of the book is simply a testimony to the challenges that lie ahead if we do not lead by example and begin building some backbone and some fight in us. We cannot teach the coming generations what we do not personally know and practice – that would make us hypocrites...

The Blessings of Brokenness[5]

Nurturing the BBTO Spirit™ means that we are first honest with ourselves. I don't believe in having life "hard" to the point where it breaks one's spirit. As a matter of fact, I strongly believe that *the purpose of difficulties is not to break your spirit but to break your will*. My will is to do whatever I want, get whatever I want, go where I want, and be whoever I choose. While we think that we can do all these things "so long as we are not hurting anyone," we fail to realize that, often, the *one* person we truly hurt is *ourselves*! When hard times come my way, I never see it as "God punishing me" but see it as "God de-wussifying me."

Comfort is a double-edged sword; it is great because we all need some R&R. My Venezuelan Latin dance partner, Michele, calls her excursions, A&R for "Austin and Relaxation" where she hikes and spends time with her brother. Whatever you call your time to "refresh" and "reboot," comfort's other edge gives us a false sense of having arrived. We begin saying things like: "It doesn't get any better than this!" In essence, mediocrity creeps in and, before we know it, we are so deep in it, we are drowning. How much of the sea should we drink before recognizing this?

<u>Notes</u>

1. *The New Webster Encyclopedic Dictionary of the English Language* (New York: Avenel Books, 1980)
2. Ecclesiastes 9:11, The Amplified Bible
3. Ecclesiastes 9:11, The New Living Translation
4. This phrase was coined by my good friend Greg Spillers
5. This heading is borrowed from the title of Dr. Charles Stanley's 1997 book, *The Blessings of Brokenness*

12. Adapt

Adapt or perish, now as ever, is nature's inexorable imperative[1]

The word "adapt" finds its origin in the Latin word *adapto*, which means "to fit[2]." It literally means "to make suitable to requirements or conditions[3]."

Bending for the Light

Chemistry and biology have always been my strong suits. Even in grade school, I loved science – mainly because of all the experiments we would do. As a naughty little boy, experiments always intrigued me because they were "something to do." One of my favorite experiments involved understanding a plant's ability to "bend" towards light when deprived of light.

The experiment involves taking a carton, cutting a small hole in it, and covering the plant with it. With only one source of light available to the plant, it begins to adapt and grow towards the light. Without boring you with the biochemical reasons and details, suffice it to say that the plant chemically and physically adapts to this sudden change in its environment. Rather than do *nothing* about this state of affairs, the plant responds by changing its "upward" plans; replacing those plans with "sideways" plans.

If plants could talk and think as we do, I am certain that the conversation would never be:

"Oh, shucks! There's no light, I can't produce food, so I guess I'll wait for someone to step up and change this terrible environment."

Rather, the plants would say:

"What?! No light?! Whatever! I have too much life in me for me to just sit here and die. I sense there's light coming in from the east corner of this environment. If the light's not going to come to me, I am going to go to it!"

If *homo sapiens* are considered to occupy the highest level of evolution and ecology, how is it possible that plants, lower in the ecology, have a more determined fight and drive in them than we do? How is it possible that other forms of life tend to recognize the need to adapt faster than we do? Do they have something in them that we do not have? Or are we simply too busy complaining about the change in environment that we cannot take some action to survive and prosper? Could it be that we have become so accustomed to being at Burger King® where we're told "Have it Your Way™?" Whatever the reason, we are in serious peril if we do not recognize the need for adapting...

Adaptation Precedes Revolution

Listening to individuals from other cultures always intrigues me. Their application of anecdotes and proverbs from their homelands into an English conversation is fascinating. One such application occurred recently when a good friend from Mexico described having four children as a revolution. "Revolución," she said in Spanish. "And nine children," I wondered? "An army," she chided.

The sociological definition of revolution is *radical and pervasive change*. Usually, such a revolution is made suddenly and accompanied by violence. In other words, it tends to be something that *must* be done. Allowing the status quo becomes such a problem that those involved have no choice but to make the change happen.

The world is getting smaller and smaller; nationalists, purists, and "patriots" are in for a rude awakening. Clothing, electronics, customer and technical services, and, now, food, are being acquired from all corners of the globe. Local companies in any region that think they cannot or will not be affected by this shrinking of the world will find themselves at the bottom of the capitalistic evolution and will become bywords like Dinosaurs...

Unless such companies are willing to adapt to this progression of life, they will soon cease to exist. And, should they continue to exist, they will be so far behind, they will never catch up. Jeff Bezos and Amazon.com were the laughing stock of business when they began; now, Barnes and Noble is wishing they had adapted to the Information Revolution – an economy and society driven heavily by the Internet.

So it is with us. Failure to adapt means we get closer and closer to extinction. *No man is born into this world whose work is not born with him*[4]. We each have a *specific* role to play during our tenure on earth. Do not traverse and leave this world having not expressed yourself fully. *There is for each man, perfect self-expression. There is a place which he is to fill and no one else can fill, something which he is to do, which no one else can do; it is his destiny!*[5]

Notes

1. H.G. Wells (1866-1946), English Writer best known for his science fiction novels *The War of the Worlds* and *The Island of Doctor Moreau*
2. *The New Webster Encyclopedic Dictionary of the English Language* (New York: Avenel Books, 1980)
3. Adapt. Dictionary.com
4. James Lowell (1819-1891), American Romantic, poet, critic, satirist, diplomat and abolitionist
5. Florence Scovel Shinn (1871-1940), *The Game of Life and How to Play It*

PART FOUR
The BBTO Commencement™

This final section of the book contains the convocation. Convocation is a summons. This is your summons to Higher Level Living™. It is your summons to the practice of beating the odds. You have been apprised of what the BBTO Spirit™ is, the Academy in which it is developed, and the necessary habits requisite for its sustenance. Now that you know the *art* of beating the odds, you will be charged with the *practice* of the art...

13. Convocation

You can't keep a squirrel down so long as timber's around -
Anonymous

Thank you for patiently wading through the waters of this small book. I am honored to have been chosen as an ambassador of good-will; one sent to you for the singular purpose of sharing a message of hope and triumph. This message has not been shared based solely on knowledge; for there are many who are more qualified than I am to bring such a message. Instead, this message has been brought to you courtesy of personal experience...

Life's been a challenge and struggle since I first broke the barrier of my mother's womb. Well into my teenage years, I was very sickly. From asthma to blood issues, I have been afflicted by many health challenges and been subject to many drug cocktails. I was told that I would not play sports like a "normal" child would because of my asthma. Socially, I was told I would not amount to much and was not worthy of many a girl or woman...

I was deeply hurt by all of these occurrences. Yet, a fire was set under me because I wanted to prove all the people that told me I wouldn't make it wrong. I did not want to give them the satisfaction of their predictions coming true. Florence Scovel Shinn was right when she said, "It takes a very strong mind to neutralize a prophecy of evil." My mind has been made stronger by the "prophecies of doom" of others. Furthermore, their prophecies became the impetus and steps I used to climb to the heights I have now climbed. I suppose it was possible for me to give in at some rough turns...

For instance, my parents gave me a roundtrip ticket and $2,000 to come to the United States. Between college tuition and fees and the cost of living, this was soon $0. Not only so, the one friend I counted on soon became a foe. So I learned how to live on the street and maintain a positive attitude while attending college and living on the street. This attitude sent the correct entreatments to the Heavens and they were opened: soon, I was living in the comfort of a home with a full-ride academic scholarship...

With a return ticket, I could easily have returned to Zambia; after all, it wasn't as though my family was doing poorly in Zambia. Yet, I knew that my complete self-expression would never occur in Zambia. I devoted myself to "Larger Purpose Thinking™" and found my way through the maze I found myself in. With every wrong turn in the maze, I learned to make better decisions and choices.

Even with better decisions and choices, challenges continued to present themselves. My passion for a higher education led me towards a master's degree program in which I was told that no one had completed the program in less than two years and my question about it was ridiculous. Again, this prophecy became the reason for triumph. I completed the degree in eight (8) months! With this triumph, it was no stretch to complete my PhD in eighteen (18) months. Not only did I complete the degree in eighteen months, my dissertation was nominated for and won the Social Change Award; an award recognizing the student and dissertation most likely to effect social change...

The challenges, I have learned, will never end; they will only intensify. Fortunately, this means that the opportunities will only increase! As of the printing of this book, I am not even 30 years old but have published two books, completed recognized research and presented my findings and other topics at national events among my peers and other diverse groups.

While this might seem like an opportunity to speak well of myself, it is meant to rouse you into action. My journey has been mostly challenging and perilous. While my dissertation and first book did well, months earlier I lost two loves: my father to kidney failure and my wife to divorce. This double-whammy could not have come at a more awkward and difficult time; yet, like my friend J Duff says: "Mother Nature doesn't have a sense of humor."

There was no advance warning; just...boom! That is the nature of life. There are few, if any, advance warnings about much. Unlike tornadoes and other adverse weather conditions using Doppler, there is no Doppler for some of the things we face in life. Sometimes without warning, a tornado (financial, emotional, physical, etc) rips the top of our home, then comes back for more and takes it all!

Yet, we rebuild. *That* is beating the odds – *rebuilding, regrouping* and being *undeterred*. We cannot be broken unless we lie on our backs after we've been knocked down. We have to get up – again! I hope that this book has given you enough to become of sterner stuff. I hope you have seen that if a farm boy from Zambia can accomplish what I have, you can as well. Resolve to accept the fact that things are going to be hard; that perils will surround you on every side. What makes you a BBTOer™ is what you become in light of these perils...

To help drive my point, consider the following story:

A young woman went to her mother and told her about her life and how things were so hard for her. She did not know how she was going to make it and wanted to give up. She was tired of fighting and struggling. It seemed as one problem was solved, a new one arose.

Her mother took her to the kitchen. She filled three pots with water and placed each one on a high fire. Soon the pots came to a boil. In the first she placed carrots, in the second she placed eggs, and in the last she placed ground coffee beans. She let them sit and boil, without saying a word.

In about twenty minutes she turned off the burners. She fished the carrots out and placed them in a bowl. She pulled the eggs out and placed them in a bowl. Then she ladled the coffee out and placed it in a bowl.

Turning to her daughter, she asked, "Tell me, what do you see?"

"Carrots, eggs, and coffee," she replied.

Her mother brought her closer and asked her to feel the carrots. She did and noted that they were soft.

The mother then asked the daughter to break one of the eggs. After pulling off the shell, she observed the hardboiled egg. Finally, the mother asked the daughter to sip the coffee.

The daughter smiled as she tasted its rich aroma. The daughter then asked, "What does it mean, Mother? What point are you trying to make?"

Her mother explained that each of these objects had faced the same adversity...boiling water.

Each reacted differently. The carrot went in strong, hard, and unrelenting. However, after being subjected to the boiling water, it softened and became weak. The egg had been fragile, its thin outer shell had protected its liquid interior, but after sitting through the boiling water, its inside became hardened. The ground coffee beans were unique, however. After they were in the boiling water, *they changed the water.*

Which one are *you*? Do the winds of adversity blow so hard that they leave you changed like the carrots and egg? Or are you resolute in your vision so much so that *you* change the situation? Whichever you are, it is never too late to make amends...

As I have tried to stress in the previous pages, there is a lot that we don't have control over. We cannot control the circumstances we find ourselves in from day to day. The only thing we can control is how we respond to each circumstance...

I, therefore, summon you to a life of productivity. One governed by "Larger Purpose Thinking™" and set on perfect self-expression. Be *fearless* in your resolve to *become*! God knew exactly what He was doing when He put you together. All you have to do now is make manifest the best of what's in you. Fight fear! It is the antithesis of faith. When you become fearless, God's work in you is complete! Have faith in yourself and believe in your perfect self-expression...

About the Author

Kozhi Sidney Makai, PhD is President and CEO of The Lectern™, an organizational behavior and development consulting firm specializing in personal and corporate performance enhancement based in The Woodlands, Texas. He is the award-winning author of *How Can I Come Up?* and award-winning researcher and author of *Culture & Leadership: A Comparison of Cultural Orientation and Leadership Preference among College Students in Zambia and the United States*. He lectures and conducts seminars for businesses and organizations across the United States and abroad, and his clients have included Coors Brewing Company, the State of Texas, and the Salvation Army.

Dr. Kozhi is a sought-after adjunct professor of organizational behavior and communication and has taught both graduate and undergraduate courses at North Harris College, Jones International University, Davenport University, and the University of Phoenix. A specialist in Interpersonal Communication, he now teaches the undergraduate course three times a year in a fast-tracked format.

His personal story of triumph, beginning in his native Zambia through five years of Premier League and International All-Nation basketball, and his academic honors made him a popular feature in publications such as the *Houston Chronicle* and the *Denver Post*. All accolades aside, Dr. Kozhi is a Social Entrepreneur who serves on several non-profit boards and devotes much time to the development of young leaders through the Leadership High School and Collegiate Leadership programs of the Community Leadership Institute as well as Phi Theta Kappa, the honor society of the two-year college.

Dr. Kozhi's life philosophy is encapsulated in the phrases *Maximizing Excellence*™ and *Question Everything*™. It is his life mission to help people "become". He holds a bachelor's degree in Speech Communication and Psychology from Sam Houston State University, a master's degree in Leadership and Influence from Jones International University, and a doctorate degree in Applied Management and Decision Sciences from Walden University.

Share BBTO™ with Others!

Helping businesses, organizations, and individuals make beating the odds a core value

Visit Dr. Makai's site for more:

www.KozhiMakai.com